OCEANS

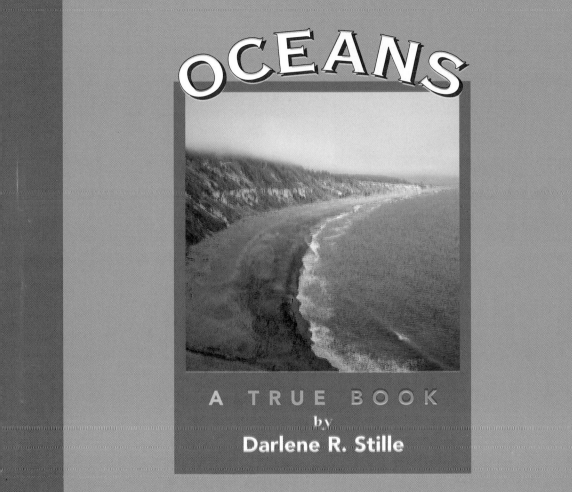

A TRUE BOOK

by

Darlene R. Stille

Children's Press®
A Division of Grolier Publishing
New York London Hong Kong Sydney
Danbury, Connecticut

Waves crashing along the coast of Oregon

Reading Consultant
Linda Cornwell
Coordinator of School Quality
and Professional Improvement
Indiana State Teachers
Association

Content Consultant
Jan Jenner, Ph.D.

Author's Dedication
For Cynthia A. Marquard,
who showed me some of the
world's great ecosystems

The photograph on the
title page shows the
California coastline.

**Visit Children's Press® on the
Internet at:
http://publishing.grolier.com**

Library of Congress Cataloging-in-Publication Data

Stille, Darlene R.
        Oceans / by Darlene R. Stille.
        p.   cm. — (A True book)
    Includes bibliographical references and index.
    Summary: An introduction to the ocean describing its physical charac-
teristics, the plants and animals that live in or near it, and its importance
to life on Earth.
    ISBN 0-516-21510-8 (lib. bdg.)   0-516-26768-x (pbk.)
    1. Oceanography—Juvenile literature. 2. Ocean—Juvenile literature.
[1. Ocean.] I. Title. II. Series.
GC21.5.S75   1999
551.46—dc21   98-53857
                                                                    CIP
                                                                    AC

GROLIER
PUBLISHING   2 3 4 5 6 7 8 9 10 R 08 07 06 05 04 03 02 01

Contents

At the Seashore   5

The World Ocean   10

Life in the Ocean   13

Coral Reefs   25

The Ocean Floor   32

The Deep Sea   35

How We Learn About the Ocean   40

To Find Out More   44

Important Words   46

Index   47

Meet the Author   48

When ocean water reaches the shore, waves crash along the beach.

At the Seashore

Have you ever been to the seashore? Did you look out over the water? No matter how far you looked, all you could see was water. Did you listen to the sound of the ocean? The sound you heard comes from the waves crashing against the beach. Did you notice that ocean water smells of salt, and it tastes very salty? This is because ocean water is salt water.

When you stepped into the water, it covered just your feet. After a few steps, the water was probably up to your knees. Soon, the water came up to your neck. Close to shore, the water is shallow. But the farther out you walk, the deeper it gets. Some parts of the ocean are thousands of feet deep!

The ocean is shallow along the beach. The farther out you walk, the deeper it gets.

If you were at the beach all day, you probably noticed that the water covered most of the beach for a few hours. This is called high tide. Most

At high tide (above), most of the beach is covered with water. At low tide (below), you can collect shells along the beach.

of the time, the water came only partway up the beach. The beach is largest at low tide. At low tide, the sand is covered with seashells and seaweeds brought in by the tide.

Ocean water is always moving. We see waves move along the top of the water. Most waves are caused by wind blowing across the ocean. Earthquakes beneath the ocean can also make waves.

The World Ocean

If you are at a beach in Rhode Island, you see the Atlantic Ocean. If you are at a beach in California, you see the Pacific Ocean. The Atlantic and the Pacific oceans are really part of one big ocean. Huge areas of land called continents break up the ocean, but every part of the ocean is connected. That is why the entire ocean is sometimes called the World Ocean.

There are different names for different parts of the World Ocean. The biggest parts of the World Ocean are called the Atlantic Ocean, the Pacific Ocean, the Indian Ocean, the Arctic Ocean, and the Antarctic Ocean. Smaller parts of the World Ocean are

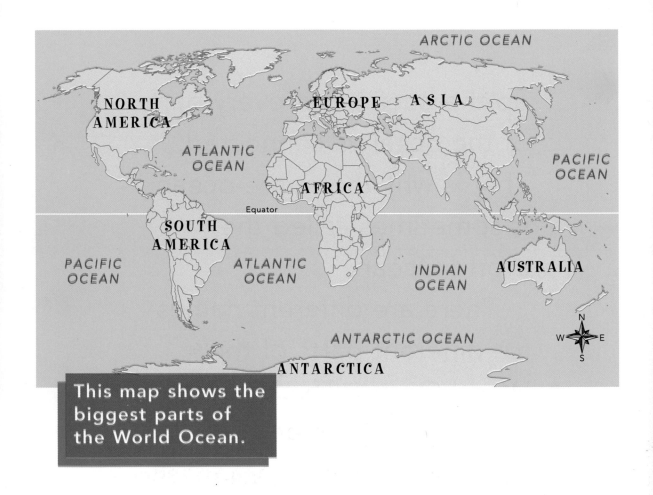

ARCTIC OCEAN

NORTH AMERICA

EUROPE   ASIA

ATLANTIC OCEAN

PACIFIC OCEAN

AFRICA

Equator

SOUTH AMERICA

PACIFIC OCEAN

ATLANTIC OCEAN

INDIAN OCEAN

AUSTRALIA

ANTARCTIC OCEAN

N
W   E
S

ANTARCTICA

This map shows the biggest parts of the World Ocean.

called seas. But sometimes people use the word "sea" when they are talking about the ocean.

Life in the Ocean

The largest animal on Earth lives in the ocean. It is the blue whale. Blue whales can be up to 100 feet (30 meters) long. Some of the smallest animals on Earth live in the ocean, too. Some plankton animals are so tiny that you need a microscope to see them.

The blue whale is the largest animal that has ever lived on Earth.

Sea jellies (left) float along the ocean's surface. These squid (below) live off the coast of southern California.

Sea jellies float on the top of the water. Tuna, cod, and other fishes swim a few feet below the surface. Deep down, there are octopuses and squid. These strange-looking animals have

The gray reef shark is a fierce hunter.

no bones, but they do have long tentacles called arms. Sharks and barracudas can be found in both deep and shallow water.

Shrimp, lobsters, and other shellfish live on the ocean's sandy floor. Sea stars, clams, sand dollars, sea urchins, and crabs sometimes live near the seashore or in tide pools.

Sand dollars (left) can be found along the ocean's sandy bottom. Giant red sea urchins (below) live off the coast of British Columbia, Canada.

A harbor seal suns itself on a rock in the Pacific Ocean.

Not all ocean animals can breathe underwater. Whales and dolphins are mammals that come up from below the surface to breathe air. Seals

A mother sea otter swims with her pup.

and sea otters are mammals that like to play in the waves. They often rest on rocks that stick above the water's surface.

Plankton contains hundreds of tiny ocean animals, algae, and bacteria. This picture was taken through a microscope.

Animals are not the only kind of living things in the ocean. There are also bacteria and algae. Like tiny ocean animals, bacteria and some algae are found in plankton. Plankton floats on or near the top of the water. Plankton is very important to all life in the ocean because many fish and other ocean animals eat it.

Larger kinds of algae are called seaweeds. Some seaweeds

Rockweed is common along the coasts of New England.

grow up from the ocean bottom. Others float in the water. Although algae are not plants, they look like plants. Algae even make food from sunlight and water—just like plants.

The biggest kind of seaweed is the giant kelp. It can be as tall as trees. Places where lots of kelps grow are called kelp forests. There is a giant kelp forest in the ocean off the coast of California.

This giant kelp grows in a kelp forest off the coast of California.

Ocean Currents

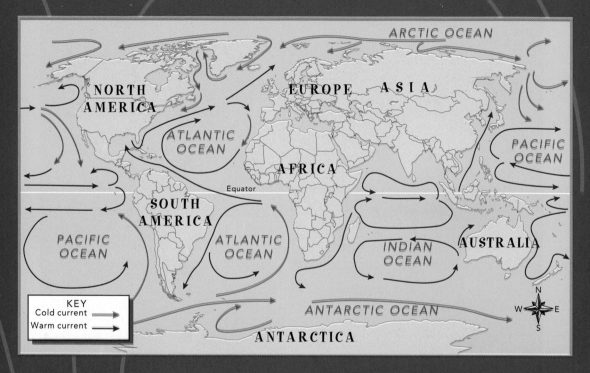

ARCTIC OCEAN

NORTH AMERICA

EUROPE ASIA

ATLANTIC OCEAN

PACIFIC OCEAN

AFRICA

Equator

SOUTH AMERICA

PACIFIC OCEAN

ATLANTIC OCEAN

INDIAN OCEAN

AUSTRALIA

KEY
Cold current
Warm current

ANTARCTIC OCEAN

ANTARCTICA

N W E S

We can see waves, but the ocean also moves in ways we cannot see. It has invisible currents. Currents are like rivers of warmer, colder, or saltier water that run through the ocean. They affect weather around the world. If the ocean water is cold, it makes the air above it cold. Warm ocean water makes the air warm.

A warm Pacific Ocean current called El Niño causes strange weather all over the world. El Niño can cause floods in some places and droughts in other places.

Coral Reefs

Coral reefs are made from the bodies of millions of tiny animals. The animals are called polyps. When these animals die, parts of their bodies turn into coral. Coral is made of limestone, which is a kind of rock. Later, a new layer of polyps grows on top of the

Some coral reefs, such as this one in the Red Sea, are brightly colored.

These soft daisy cup polyps grow off the coast of Australia.

limestone. As polyps continue to grow, die, and turn into limestone, the coral reef gets bigger and bigger.

These hard corals have attracted dozens of lyretail fairy basslets.

Some kinds of coral are hard, and some kinds are soft. Coral reefs are made from hard corals. The polyps that form hard coral can live only in water that is warm all year round. That is why coral reefs are found near the equator.

Corals can have different shapes. One kind of soft coral looks like a fan waving in the

These colorful gorgonian sea fans grow in the South Pacific. They are a type of soft coral.

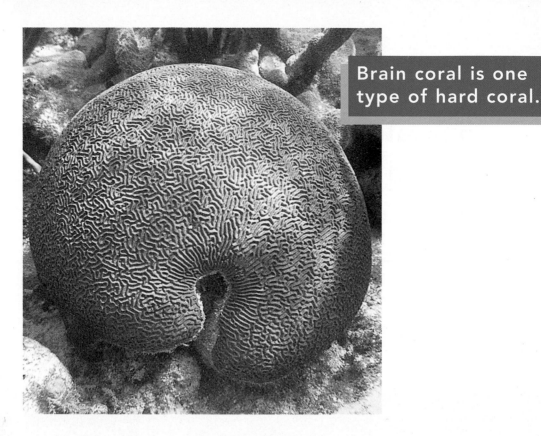

water. Hard corals can look like antlers, branches, mushrooms—or even like a brain.

Many different kinds of animals live on coral reefs. Colorful tropical fish swim in and out of the coral. Sea urchins and sea anemones cling to the hard coral. Clams, sponges, and sea horses also live on coral reefs.

A coral reef off the coast of Papua New Guinea

The Ocean Floor

We think of the ocean bottom as being flat and sandy. That is how it is near shore. But as the ocean floor slopes down, it becomes very different!

If you could go down to the deepest parts of the ocean, you would see tall mountains, wide valleys, and flat plains.

The landscape of the ocean floor includes mountains, valleys, and plains.

You would also see volcanoes shooting out hot melted rock and geysers spraying hot water. In some places along the ocean floor, melted rock

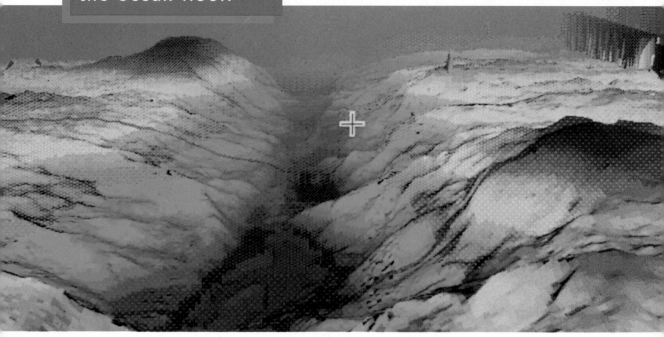

oozes up through deep cracks called trenches. This hot rock comes from inside Earth. When it cools, the rock forms new ocean floor.

The Deep Sea

The deepest part of the ocean is in the Pacific Ocean. It is almost 7 miles (11.3 kilometers) to the bottom! Deep down, the water is very dark because light from the sun cannot go this deep into the water. Since there is no sunlight, algae cannot live in the deep sea.

Deep-sea animals, such as these copepods, eat materials that drift down from the ocean surface.

What do deep-sea animals eat? When animals that live near the surface of the ocean die, their bodies fall toward the ocean floor. Many deep-sea animals catch and eat the dead bodies.

Many deep-sea animals, such as this fish and comb jelly, glow in the dark.

The animals that live in the deep sea look strange to us. Some have no eyes. Others make their own light. Their bodies have chemicals that make them glow in the dark.

Many animals have other special features that help them live in the dark, cold waters of the deep ocean.

Some deep-sea animals live near underwater geysers that spray hot water and other materials into the ocean. Here you will find clams and chocolate-colored mussels the size of footballs. Huge white crabs run along the ocean floor. Giant tubeworms with red tops move with the currents.

These twin deep-sea geysers (above) spout hot water full of chemicals. Tubeworms, crabs, and mussels (right) are a few of the animals that live close to the geysers.

How We Learn About the Ocean

Scientists study the ocean in many ways. They use ships and satellites. They have instruments that float on the waves. But the most exciting way to learn about the ocean is by diving into the deep waters. For this, they use special submarines.

A scientist lowers a thermometer into the ocean.

Alvin has made many trips to the deepest parts of the ocean.

Alvin is a little white submarine that has made many discoveries. *Alvin* has powerful lights for seeing in the dark. It also has an "arm" for picking up objects on the ocean floor.

Scientists ride in *Alvin* and other submarines. But they also use robot submarines with TV cameras on board. Scientists are learning more and more about the ocean every year.

To Find Out More

Here are some additional resources to help you learn more about oceans:

 **Books**

Kerrod, Robin. **Learn About the Sea.** Anness Publishing, 1998.

Meister, Carl. **The Ocean.** ABDO Publishing, 1999.

Savage, Stephen. **Animals of the Oceans.** Raintree Steck-Vaughn, 1997

Taylor, Leighton R. **Creeps from the Deep.** Chronicle Books, 1997.

Waterlow, Julia. **The Atlantic Ocean.** Raintree Steck-Vaughn, 1997

Wood, Jakki. **Across the Big Blue Sea: An Ocean Wildlife Book.** National Geographic Society, 1998.

Organizations and Online Sites

Alaska SeaLife Center
*http://www.alaskasealife.org
/index.html*

Contains stories about individual animals living at the center.

Deep Sea World
*http://www.deepseaworld.
com/*

The National Aquarium of Scotland features a virtual tour of the deep.

**Great Barrier
Reef Aquarium**
*http://aquarium.gbrmpa.
gov.au/*

Many pictures of coral reefs and animals that live at the aquarium.

**International Year of the
Ocean — Kids' and
Teachers' Resources**
*http://www.yoto98.noaa.
gov/kids.htm*

Activities and facts about oceans, climate, and endangered marine animals. The site is manitained by the National Oceanographic and Atmospheric Administration.

**Monterey Bay
Aquarium Online**
http://www.mbayaq.org/

See a live image of the Giant Kelp Forest exhibit from a camera mounted inside.

Ocean Schoolyard
*http://www.oceanscanada.
com/IYO/eng/index.htm*

Fun facts about the ocean and ocean animals, sponsored by the International Year of the Ocean, Canada.

**Underwater World
Singapore**
*http://www.
underwaterworld.com.sg/*

Features a virtual tour of the exhibits at this oceanarium in Asia.

**World Wildlife Federation
Celebrates the Year of the
Ocean**
*http://www.wwf.org/yoto/
yoto.htm*

Facts about ocean habitats and threats to various species.

45

Important Words

algae living things that look similar to plants and make their own food

coral reef an ocean formation made from the bodies of tiny animals called polyps

current a river of warmer, colder, or saltier water that runs through the ocean

evaporation ocean water that rises into the air as water vapor and falls back to Earth as rain or snow

mammal an animal that has a backbone and feeds its young with mother's milk

plankton tiny plants and animals that float on or near the top of the ocean water

polyp a tiny ocean animal that turns into limestone when it dies and forms coral reefs

Index

(**Boldface** page numbers
indicate illustrations.)

algae, 20–22, **20,** 35, 46
bacteria, 20, **20**
coral reef, 25, **26,** 27–31,
31, 46
corals, 28–30, **28, 29, 30**
currents, 24, **24,** 46
deep sea, 6, 16, 35–38,
36, 37, 39, 42
deep sea animals, 36–38,
36, 37, 39
El Niño, 24
evaporation, 24, 46
fish, 15–16, **16,** 21, 30,
31, **37**
geysers, 33, 38, **39**
kelp forests, 22, **23**
limestone, 25, 27, 46
mammals, 18–19, **18, 19,**
46

marine animals, 13, **14,**
15, **15,** 17–21, **17–20,**
25, 30–31
ocean floor, 32–34, **33,**
34, 36, 43
ocean names, 10, 11, 12,
12, 24, 35
plankton, 13, 20–21, **20,**
46
polyps, 25, 27–28, **27,** 46
scientists, 40, **41,** 43
seas, 12, **26**
seaweed, 9, 21, **21,** 22
shellfish, 17, 31, 38, **39**
submarine, 40, **41, 42,** 43
tides, 7, **8,** 9, 17
trench, 34, **34**
waves, **2, 4,** 5, 9, 19, 24,
40
weather, 24
whales, 13, **14,** 18
World Ocean, 10, 11, **12**

Meet the Author

Darlene R. Stille lives in Chicago, Illinois, and is executive editor of the World Book Annuals and World Book's Online Service. She has written many books for Children's Press, including *Extraordinary Women Scientists*, *Extraordinary Women of Medicine*, four True Books about the human body, and four other True Books about ecosystems.

Photographs ©: Alice Alldredge: 36; Dembinsky Photo Assoc.: 2 (Willard Clay), 8 top (Greg Gawlowski), 7 (Mark E. Gibson), 1 (Adam Jones), 16 (Marilyn Kazmers), 26 (Mark J. Thomas); ENP Images: 8 bottom, 18, 19, 27 (Gerry Ellis); Galaxy Contact/Explorer: 33; Peter Girguis: 37 left; Photo Researchers: 14 (Francois Gohier), 28, 31 (David Hall), 17 bottom (Andrew J. Martinez), 15 bottom (Gregory Ochocki), 41 (Jan Robert Factor), 29 (F. Stuart Westmorland), 20 (D. P. Wilson/Science Source); Superstock, Inc.: cover ; Verena Tunnicliffe: 39 top (University of Victoria, BC.); Visuals Unlimited: 23 (Hal Beral), 37 right (Robert Degoursey), 4 (Don W. Fawcett), 15 top (William Jorgensen), 30 (Keogh), 17 top (A. Kerstitch), 21 (Science VU), 39 bottom (WHOI/D. Foster); Woods Hole Oceanographic Institution: 42 (WHOI/Rod Catanach), 34.
Maps by Bob Italiano.